I0605338

JOB DISCOVERY

JOBS IF YOU LIKE SOCIAL MEDIA

by Roxanne Troup

BrightPoint Press

San Diego, CA

an imprint of ReferencePoint Press, Inc.
Printed in the United States

For more information, contact:
BrightPoint Press
PO Box 27779
San Diego, CA 92198
www.BrightPointPress.com

LIBRARY OF CONGRESS CATALOGING-IN-PUBLICATION DATA

Names: Troup, Roxanne, author.
Title: Jobs if you like social media / by Roxanne Troup.
Description: San Diego, CA: BrightPoint Press, [2025] | Series: Job discovery | Includes bibliographical references and index. | Audience: Grades 7–9
Identifiers: LCCN 2024004127 (print) | LCCN 2024004128 (eBook) | ISBN 9781678209186 (hardcover) | ISBN 9781678209193 (eBook)
Subjects: LCSH: Social media--Vocational guidance--Juvenile literature.
Classification: LCC HM742.T77 2025 (print) | LCC HM742 (eBook) | DDC 302.23/1023--dc23/eng/20240318
LC record available at https://lccn.loc.gov/2024004127
LC eBook record available at https://lccn.loc.gov/2024004128

CONTENTS

THE SOCIAL MEDIA INDUSTRY AT A GLANCE

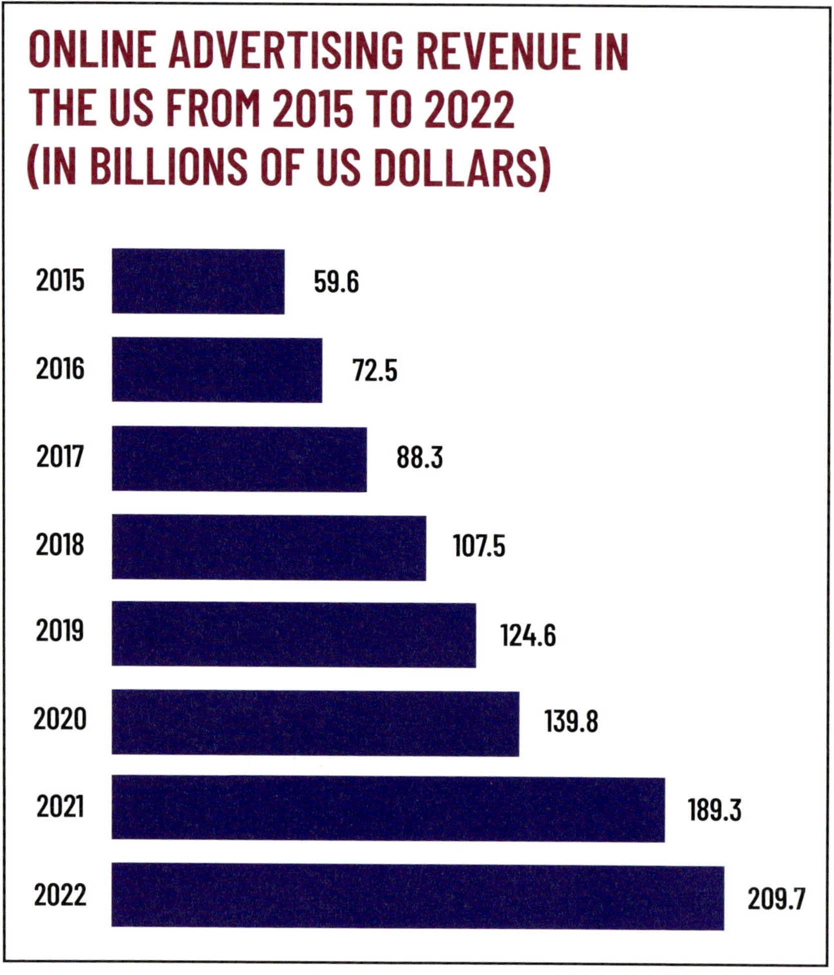

Source: "Online Advertising Revenue in the United States from 2000 to 2022," Statista, *April 2023. www.statista.com.*

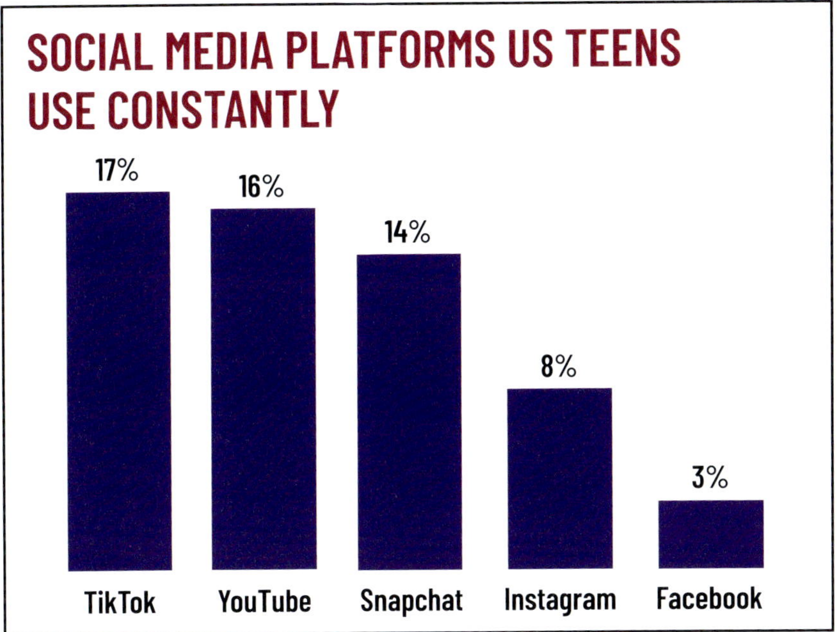

Source: Monica Anderson, Michelle Faverio, and Jeffrey Gottfried, "Teens, Social Media and Technology 2023," Pew Research Center, *December 11, 2023. www.pewresearch.org.*

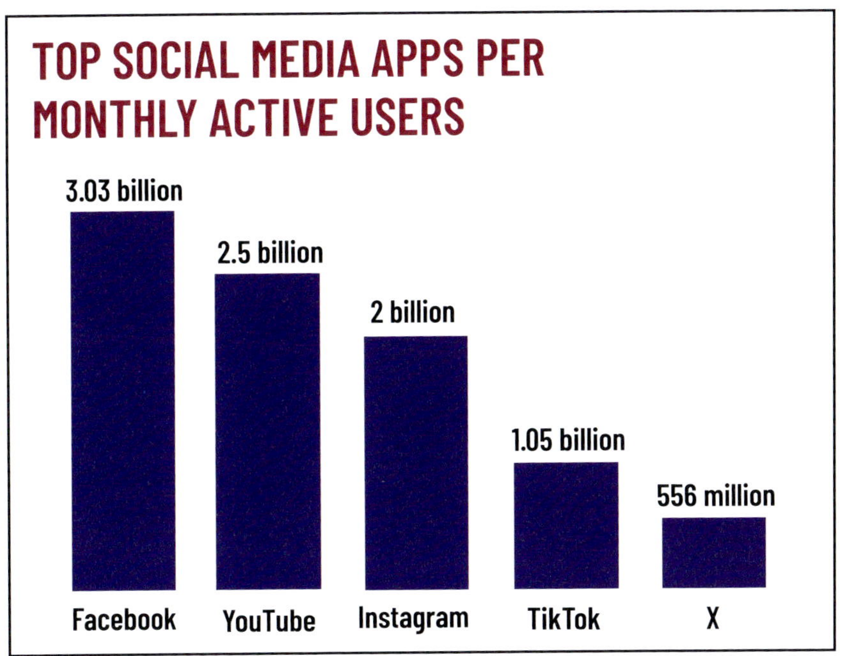

Source: Tamilore Oladipo. "23 Top Social Media Sites to Consider for Your Brand in 2024," Buffer, *November 20, 2023. www.buffer.com.*

SOCIAL MEDIA: THE GREAT CONNECTOR

More than one million new books are published in the United States each year. This can make it hard to find an audience for any given book. But BookTok is changing that. BookTok is a community of book lovers on TikTok. TikTok is a social media **platform**. BookTok creators make short videos to recommend their favorite books. Sometimes those videos

Social media influencers create videos about their favorite hobbies or activities.

go viral. When this happens, a book's sales can skyrocket.

In 2021, BookToker Sarah Scannell discovered an old murder mystery. *Cain's Jawbone* was first published in 1934. The author wrote the book as a puzzle. The book contains clues. But its pages are bound out of order. To solve the mystery, readers must put the book's pages in the correct order. This helps them figure out which clues to follow.

Sarah hoped to solve the mystery. She cut out the pages and taped them to her bedroom wall. She pieced the clues together. Sarah shared her *Cain's Jawbone* wall on BookTok. It went viral. Bookstores sold out of the book. The publisher rushed to reprint it. As of 2023, more than

BookTok was started by TikTok users who love books.

500,000 copies of the book have sold since it was reprinted in 2019. But Sarah had yet to solve the puzzle. Publisher John Mitchinson credits her with the book's success. "I really didn't expect [so many] people to be joining me in this activity," Sarah said in an interview. "I'm just here to have fun on my own time."[1]

WHAT IS THE SOCIAL MEDIA INDUSTRY?

Sarah uses social media to connect with others with similar interests. Platforms like

Influencers can inspire followers to buy products, such as books.

TikTok can also link customers to products. The money people make and spend on these products drives the social media industry. Sarah Scannell influenced others to buy *Cain's Jawbone*. This made her part of the social media industry.

The social media industry includes many different jobs. Influencers like Sarah are part of the industry. Content creators, social media managers, and customer service representatives work in the industry, too. Digital forensics investigator is another social media career. Investigators look for connections between social media use and crime. These are just a few of the careers available in the social media industry.

CHAPTER ONE

CONTENT CREATOR

Content creators share experiences on social media. They entertain and inform. Content creators craft content and post it online. Content can be articles or social media posts. It can also be images or videos. Some creators make content for their own platforms. Others are hired by businesses. They produce content for that company's brand. Brands are products and services tied to a certain name.

Content creators do everything from making videos to writing blog posts. Their goal is to engage and entertain their followers.

Content creators can **freelance** or work as employees.

Some content creators write. They post blogs or craft video scripts. Others write copy for websites or emails. Copy is the words written to sell something. Nearly every word on business websites was written by someone. Other content creators design graphics. They edit

Content Creator

Education: None required

Personal Qualities: Creative, an excellent communicator, resourceful, efficient

Working Conditions: Content creators work mostly indoors on a computer.

Average Salary: $61,988

photos and animate doodles. Some make **infographics**. Their designs are used in articles and on social media. Other creators make videos.

Some content creators are influencers like Sarah Scannell. These people have loyal followers on social media. People see some influencers as experts. Other influencers inspire their followers. Sometimes an influencer will recommend a product or service. Many of their followers may buy the product.

TRAINING AND SKILLS

Independent content creators do not need a college degree. But learning video editing and writing skills can be useful. Taking design and marketing classes may be helpful as well. They help creators find and connect with their target audience. These courses are offered at different colleges. They are also offered through online platforms. Some platforms include Skillshare, HubSpot, and Coursera.

Content creators must be great communicators. Creativity is important, too. Some content creators work for one company. Others are freelancers.

Silent But Memorable

In 2020, Khaby Lame began posting videos on TikTok. He made fun of complicated life hacks. But he never said a word. He just showed viewers an easier way to do things. In September 2023, Khaby became the most popular creator on TikTok. Over 161 million people follow him.

Learning how to use video editing programs can be a great addition to a content creator's skill set.

Freelance creators work for many different companies. They must set their own schedules and fees. This means business skills are helpful.

HOW TO GET STARTED

Independent content creators must build a following. This means they need a unique way of sharing ideas. "Readers click on your

Influencers build a loyal following by providing a lot of quality content with a specific theme.

content for the information, but they come back for the personality,"[2] says marketing expert Maggie Butler.

The hardest part of the job is finding an audience. Most successful content creators do this by focusing on a specific niche. A niche is a small part of the market.

Some might share their cooking expertise. Others post technology reviews. The key is to target posts to a specific need within the market. Creators might make only chocolate dessert recipes. That focus is their niche.

Vanessa Lau is a creator who posts on social media. Lau says the best way to find a niche is to experiment. She explains, "The mistake that I see a lot of aspiring content creators making is they stress so much about finding a niche to the point where they don't create any content at all."[3] She encourages new creators to start small. Set a schedule and post content consistently. Also track how people respond to content. Tools such as Google Analytics can help. Then create more of the content that people like.

FUTURE DIRECTIONS

In 2023 the creator economy was a $250 billion industry. Goldman Sachs Research predicts that this number will double by 2027. But few creators earn a full salary. Niche creators are an exception. They are able to influence followers to buy the products they recommend. Businesses like this. These creators may be able to earn higher incomes from corporate sponsorships.

Constantly improving technology makes it easier to create quality content. Editing is faster. Design software is easier to learn. But social media platforms will continue to change. For example, when YouTube first appeared, it was the king of video. Then TikTok became popular.

YouTube responded. The platform changed how it delivered content to viewers. It listed shorter videos first in searches. Content creators adapted their content to these changes.

New technology could also create more competition. Since 2023, creators have

When content creators gain a large enough following, companies may offer them samples of products to post about and recommend to their audience.

used **artificial intelligence** (AI). They use it to research keywords. Some use it to edit content. Others use it to add captions to videos. AI is cheap and fast. But it is not creative. It can only make what humans tell it to make. As technology improves, that could change. But most experts believe AI should not replace the creative process.

Influencers and content creators must keep up with the latest features offered by social media platforms to produce posts that are popular with followers.

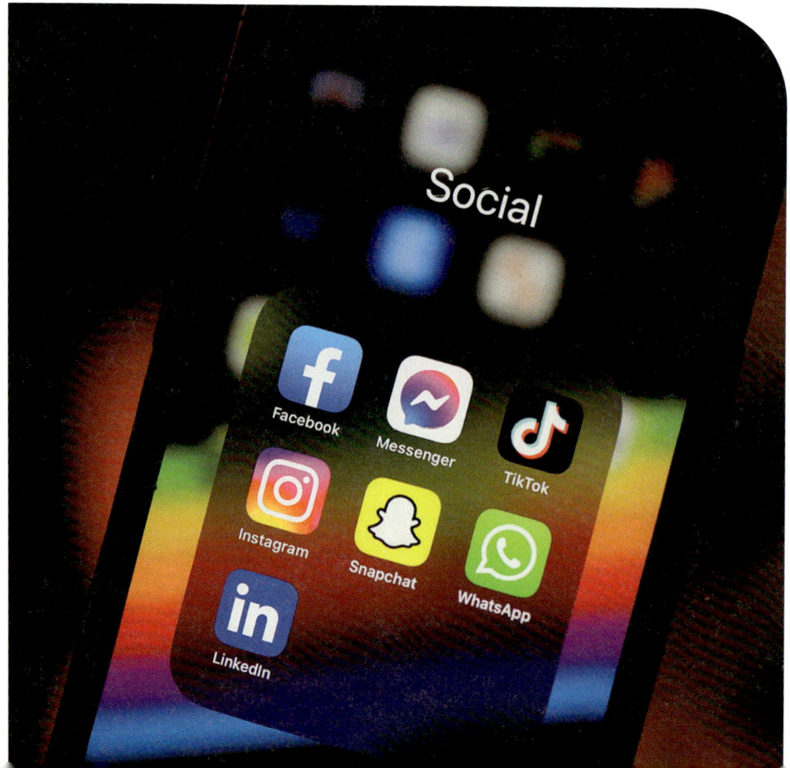

FIND OUT MORE

Coursera

www.coursera.org

Coursera is an online learning platform. It offers over 5,800 courses, certificates, and degrees from schools around the world. Most of their courses are free. But students who pass the final exam can pay a small fee for certification or college credit.

Exploding Topics

www.explodingtopics.com

Exploding Topics is a tool that tracks what people search for online. It helps content creators determine which topics internet users are most interested in. It also provides businesses with keywords and phrases to add to their marketing content. This can improve search results.

CHAPTER TWO

SOCIAL MEDIA MANAGER

Social media (SM) managers oversee marketing campaigns. They may work with a team of content creators to help companies connect with customers. They use a client's social media accounts to promote the client's brand. Brands can be linked to companies, such as Nike. Or they can represent a person.

An SM manager also builds relationships with clients. They are the contact person

Social media managers work with creative team members to come up with successful marketing plans.

between the client and the creative team. They engage with customers, too. SM managers tell stories to help customers remember the client. This is called building brand awareness. Hugo Molinaro is a marketing expert. He says, "Social media is generally considered . . . the first interaction a user has with your brand. Thus, most

Social Media Manager

Education: 4-year degree or certificate program

Personal Qualities: Creative, analytical, organized, a good communicator, familiar with social media platforms, a good decision-maker

Working Conditions: Social media managers work on a computer in a home or business office.

Average Salary: $58,164

marketers agree that successful social media campaigns focus on growing brand awareness."[4]

Some SM managers create the content brands share. Others decide how and when to post the content their client provides. Managers may post content in many different places online. Others specialize in one type of media. They may focus on Facebook campaigns. Or they could market themselves as TikTok experts.

SM managers use software to keep track of the number of likes or shares a post receives. The software also tracks how often users click on a post to visit the website. This information helps a business know how well a post is connecting to its audience.

TRAINING AND SKILLS

There are many ways to become a social media manager. Some people earn a 4-year degree. They study public relations, marketing, or business. Other people choose a certificate program. These students take one course at a time.

Social Media: Powerful and Unpredictable

Social media can be unpredictable. *Star Wars* actress Carrie Fisher died in 2016. The fast-food chain Cinnabon posted a picture on social media in her honor. They used a cinnamon bun to recreate her famous hairstyle from the movie series. Many people did not like that. They thought Cinnabon was trying to profit from someone's death.

In marketing classes, students learn how to identify their audience and come up with marketing strategies.

Students earn a certificate of completion when they pass the final exam. LinkedIn Learning, HubSpot, and Coursera offer marketing courses and certificates.

Students in these programs study different social platforms. Digital marketers must know which platforms their customers prefer. They also need to know what type of content is best for that platform. Students learn marketing strategy.

The ability to design and sketch concepts can help social media managers communicate their marketing ideas.

They study content creation. And they learn about digital communications.

SM managers must be organized. They need design skills. When creating or approving content, the brand look must be consistent. Also, SM managers must be flexible. New tools and platforms are developed each year. They need to be willing to learn new skills.

HOW TO GET STARTED

Most SM management jobs require experience. Many colleges partner with companies to provide student internships. These are temporary jobs. They provide valuable work experience. An internship with a marketing or social media company is especially helpful. Interns learn how to identify a target audience. Sometimes internships turn into full-time jobs.

Students also need to create a portfolio. Portfolios contain examples of a person's work. They can be physical or digital. A good portfolio has sample designs and case studies. A case study looks at

Creating a strong portfolio with a variety of work samples is key to landing a job in social media management.

how a business grew because of an SM manager's work. Students can build their portfolios with work from marketing classes or internships.

Students with some experience and a portfolio can apply for entry-level jobs. These include jobs such as a marketing assistant or a digital content creator. In these jobs, students learn organization and creative skills.

FUTURE DIRECTIONS

In 2023, nearly 4.9 billion people used social media. Most of them used many platforms. Businesses want to reach these customers. This means the demand for social media managers is increasing. Marketing director Julie Meredith explains. "It's clear that social media marketing isn't just an option anymore," she says. "It's a business-critical operation."[5] SM managers must decide which platforms work best for their clients.

The gig economy is changing SM management. Workers in the gig economy

Thinking of ways to best reach an audience is an important part of an SM manager's job.

earn wages with short-term contracts called gigs. These workers are not company employees. They work for themselves. Often they complete projects for several businesses. Workers in the gig economy are freelancers or independent contractors. A laptop and internet access allows them to work anywhere.

FIND OUT MORE

American Marketing Association (AMA)
www.ama.org
The AMA is a community for professional marketers. Its website provides industry news and training. It also offers certification programs and resources for college students.

The Digital Marketing Association
www.dmaglobal.com
The Digital Marketing Association's website provides members with certification in digital marketing and social media. It also offers users continuing education opportunities, links to helpful resources, and industry news.

Digital Marketing Institute
www.digitalmarketinginstitute.com
The Digital Marketing Institute is an online learning platform that provides resources and education for online marketers. Most courses are self-paced and can be completed in just a few weeks.

CHAPTER THREE

CUSTOMER SERVICE REPRESENTATIVE

Customer service is changing. More customers are looking for help online. These channels are faster than calling and emailing. This can result in happier customers.

A FedEx Office customer posted a complaint on X. This is the platform that used to be called Twitter. He was not home to sign for his delivery. The nearest pickup location was over an hour away. A social

Customer service representatives answer calls, respond to online messaging, and answer emails.

media customer care representative, or rep, saw his message. The customer had his package the next day.

Twenty-four percent of customers use social media to research products before buying. They watch video **tutorials**. They ask other customers for help.

Customer Service Representative

Education: Mostly on-the-job training

Personal Qualities: An excellent communicator, a good problem-solver, empathetic, calm under pressure

Working Conditions: Customer service representatives work in an office setting, on a computer.

Average Salary: $37,780

Many customers use the live chat feature on company websites to ask questions or resolve issues.

Customer relations expert Brent Leary says, "By building out a strong . . . online presence, businesses have an opportunity to collaborate and leverage creator communities and social platforms that . . . provide more genuine buying and service experiences."[6] Many companies hire staff to help customers. These service reps work through social media.

Customer service reps follow a company's social media channels. They answer customer questions. They respond to reviews and address complaints. Sometimes they even issue refunds.

TRAINING AND SKILLS

Customer service reps do not need a college degree. They do need good communication skills. Reps are good problem solvers. They must be patient

The Silent Ones

According to a February 2023 survey, 91 percent of unhappy customers never complain. They simply stop doing business with a company. Brands rely on the few who do complain. Their feedback helps companies learn how to improve their services.

with customers. Good customer service reps don't give excuses. They find answers.

Customer service managers have several years of experience. Most also have a 4-year degree. Many study business administration or hospitality. These degrees teach leadership and customer care. Managers learn how to train staff. Managers may choose to become certified instead. The Customer Service Institute of America offers some options.

Customer service team members learn on the job. They learn the software they will use. Team members also study the company's products. They learn how to talk to customers. Training teaches team members to adapt. It helps them feel like they are part of a team.

Customer service reps are trained in the software and platforms they need to succeed at their jobs.

HOW TO GET STARTED

Customer service is often considered an entry-level job. This means it doesn't require experience. Many people apply for these positions. A good **cover letter** can help applicants stand out.

Applicants should prepare for the job interview. They should understand the basics of the job. They should know about the company. During the interview, they should try to connect their skills and past experiences to the job. For example, those who speak more than one language should mention it in the interview. This is a skill that allows them to help more customers.

FUTURE DIRECTIONS

Many reports indicate that the need for customer service reps is diminishing. With AI-driven chatbots, companies can respond instantly to customer questions. Customers can find many answers to common questions online. AI can even help customer service reps respond. It uses predictive text. This speeds up the customer service process. But human reps are still needed.

Whether job interviews are in person or virtual, they give the employer a sense of the applicant's communication skills and knowledge about the job.

Problems that require creative solutions need human agents.

Some companies choose to serve their customers with only human agents. This makes them stand out from their competition. Others use a combination of AI and human customer representatives. The customer care industry is huge. Many jobs will continue to be available in the future.

FIND OUT MORE

The Future of Commerce
www.the-future-of-commerce.com
The Future of Commerce website is a source for industry news and commentary. This site has articles about business marketing, technology trends, and e-commerce customer service.

National Customer Service Association
www.nationalcsa.com
NCSA helps businesses develop customer service policies. It also provides employee training and certification.

The Social Media Association
www.thesocialmediaassociation.com
The Social Media Association sets ethical and legal standards for those who use social media for business. It provides members with education seminars. It also posts current job listings.

CHAPTER FOUR

DIGITAL FORENSIC INVESTIGATOR

Forensics is the science of studying evidence to solve crimes. Digital forensics is the study of electronic evidence. Law enforcement uses forensics to evaluate evidence. This can be used to stop crime. It can also be used to prove whether a suspect is guilty or not. Digital forensic investigators recover information from computers and smartphones. They collect data from email and social media sites.

Digital forensic investigators examine evidence gathered from cell phones, computers, and social media accounts.

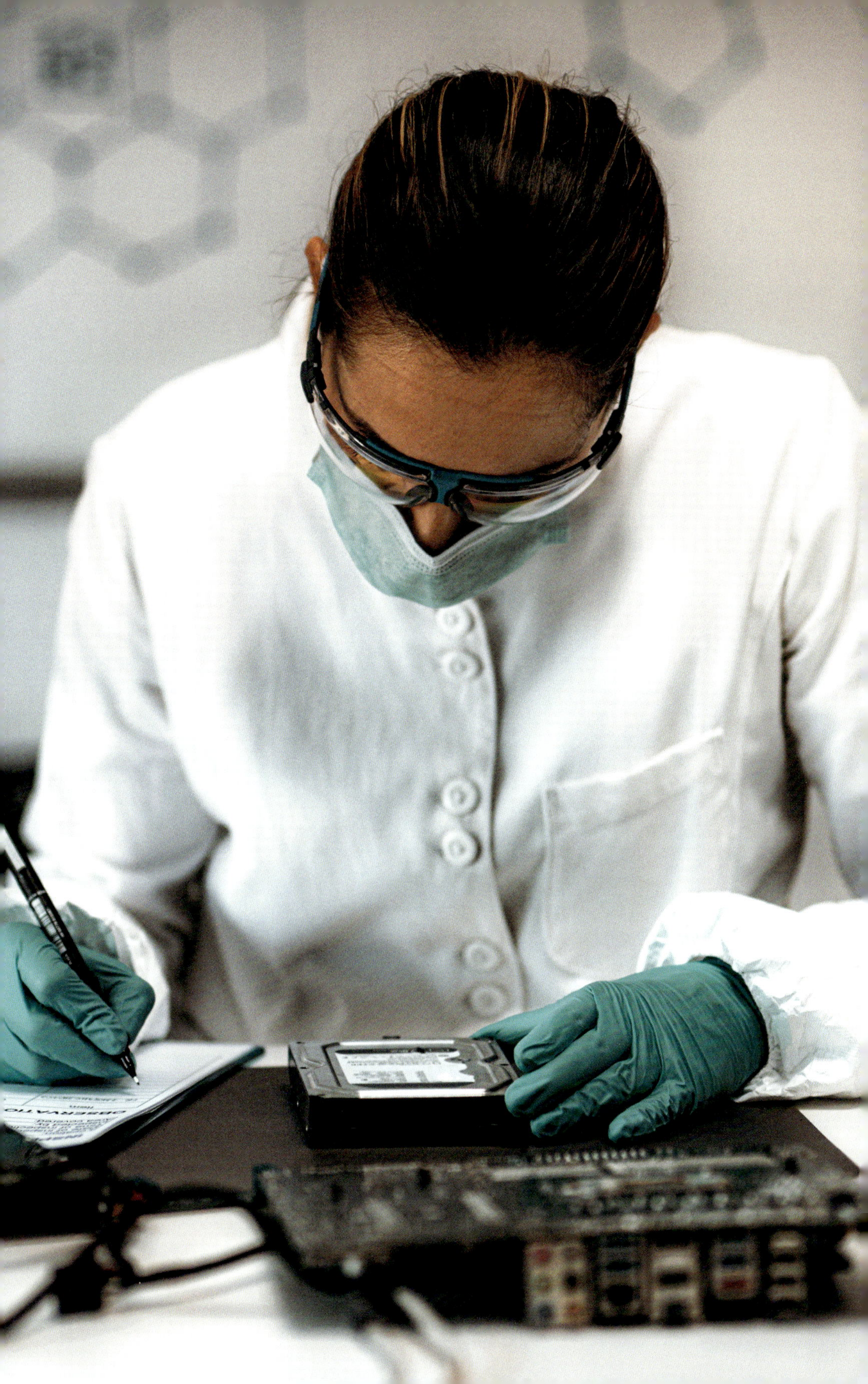

This information is studied and presented in court.

In 2016, a man was arrested in Indianapolis, Indiana. He planned a robbery. It failed, but he shot a person at the scene. Police found the man's fingerprint at

Digital Forensic Investigator

Education: 4-year degree in criminal justice or computer science

Personal Qualities: Analytical, objective, questioning, calm under pressure, adaptable

Licenses & Certificates: May require a certificate in cybersecurity

Working Conditions: Digital forensic investigators work mostly in an office setting, at a computer.

Average Salary: $70,000

the scene. They also found a bullet. But this wasn't enough to connect the man to the crime. They turned to digital forensic investigators. They found a note the man sent about the crime to his stepbrother using Facebook Messenger. Investigators kept looking. The man had used the Offer Up app to arrange the meeting where the robbery occurred. The investigators were able to track the messages to his phone. He was found guilty of the crime and sent to prison.

Investigators use different tools to study digital evidence. Some tools uncover hidden data. Others copy data for later use. There are also tools to help process images. Some tools recover old emails and internet search histories. There are even tools that

Evidence, such as hard drives, must be carefully documented and handled during investigations.

track devices connected to a computer or network.

Digital forensic investigators must follow rules. This means they must keep excellent records. They note who collected the evidence. Investigators must document where the evidence was found. They need to include data on how it was collected. When necessary, they create a digital copy of it. These records are part of a

chain of custody for the evidence. It proves to a judge and jury that the evidence is genuine.

TRAINING AND SKILLS

For most digital forensic investigators, a 4-year degree is the first step. Statistics and computer science are common majors. These degrees build advanced math and science skills. These skills help investigators recognize patterns and collect data. Tech skills are also important. Understanding code and **metadata** are key. Psychology classes help investigators understand human behavior.

Others start by studying criminal justice. These people attend a police academy. They serve a few years on the force.

Then they train to become a certified computer examiner. They earn a certificate in cybersecurity. They learn to research and analyze data.

HOW TO GET STARTED

A career in digital forensics requires experience. Students gain some experience

Some digital forensic investigators start with degrees in computer science.

in college. Classes with labs provide hands-on experience. Students can also look for internships. Cybersecurity or intelligence internships are ideal. The Department of Justice offers internships. The Department of Homeland Security does as well. Companies that contract with the government are also a good fit.

Intelligence in the Digital Age

Intelligence is information gathering. Police, military, and government officials use it to prevent and prosecute crime. The oldest way to gather information is through human interaction. This is HUMINT, or human intelligence. One of the newest ways is through social media or SOCMINT. It collects information people post online.

Capture the Flag (CTF) events are another way to gain experience. CTF is an online **simulation**. Players look for text strings called flags. These are hidden in websites or programs. This allows students to practice their cybersecurity skills. Tim Nary is a security engineer. He recommends CTF for students. “CTF teaches you to learn on the fly, and work with technologies and systems you might not have used before,” Nary says. “You have to outthink someone who’s trying to stop you from doing what you’re doing.”[7]

CTF events like Netwars test a person’s ability to find digital clues. Participants discover hidden files. Then they recover files that have been deleted. They also analyze **encrypted** data. Capture the Flag teaches

Organized hacking competitions allow companies to find the weaknesses in their computer systems. This allows them to improve their cybersecurity to prevent attacks.

technical skills. It also teaches critical thinking and problem-solving skills.

FUTURE DIRECTIONS

Digital forensics is a growing career. More people are relying on the internet and digital technologies. This increases the need for digital evidence. Government agencies and private companies regularly hire investigators. They try to protect databases from cyberattacks. Most digital forensic work happens in a crime lab. Police also investigate digital crimes.

The increase in technology use makes digital forensics more challenging. It takes longer to examine the data. It can also be hard to determine if evidence is useful or trustworthy. But AI can help. Law enforcement works with universities to develop new AI technology. AI speeds up the processing of data. It can search images and videos for faces. It can also scan computer networks that connect multiple devices. But human investigators are still needed. They can help explain and provide context for what specific evidence might mean.

FIND OUT MORE

Department of Justice Programs
www.ojp.gov
At the Department of Justice (DOJ) website, search "digital forensics" to discover all that the DOJ is doing in the field. Read DOJ articles, watch video interviews, and learn about new technologies.

Federal Law Enforcement Training Centers
www.fletc.gov
The Federal Law Enforcement Training Centers offer career-long training for law enforcement officers, including those who work in digital forensics. The website is the best place to learn about upcoming conferences geared specifically toward law enforcement.

OTHER JOBS IN THE SOCIAL MEDIA INDUSTRY

Community Manager

Community managers are brand ambassadors. They work as part of a company's marketing team. Their job is to help brands create community online. Like a social media manager, they want people to know how great their brand is. But instead of creating posts as the company, they engage as a real person. They use a personal account to talk with customers. They ask questions and find out what customers want. Then they pass this information to the marketing team so the company can meet that need.

Social Media Consultant

Social media consultants help clients improve their presence on social media. Consultants may set up accounts for the client on multiple platforms. They could develop strategies for how to grow each account. They could also update a client's accounts. Consultants may teach a client how to write good posts. Most social media consultants do freelance work. They only work with a client for a short time.

Software Developer

Software developers create new apps and computer software. They design and build games, computer programs, and web applications. Most software developers study computer science. They create open-source and proprietary programs. Open-source programs can be used for free, and the person using them can make changes. Proprietary programs are usually owned by a company. People can pay to use them, but they cannot make changes to them.

Social SEO Specialist

SEO means search engine optimization. Writers who specialize in SEO add keywords to their online content. Search engines catalog these keywords. When someone searches a keyword, the search engine provides a list of websites that use that word. The more keywords a website uses, the higher the website ranks in that list. Social SEO specialists use this same technique to add keywords to social media posts. This makes it easier for users to find brand content in a search.

GLOSSARY

artificial intelligence

the ability of a computer to do tasks usually done by humans

chain of custody

the tracking of evidence through the process of collection, storage, and analysis

encrypted

data that is hidden by a password or changed into a code

freelance

work a person does independently for a variety of clients

infographics

charts or diagrams used to share information

metadata

information about a set of data

platform

an online gathering place for people to socialize and network

simulation

a model based on a real situation or process that is used for training purposes

tutorials

step-by-step explanations of tasks, usually in video form

SOURCE NOTES

INTRODUCTION: SOCIAL MEDIA: THE GREAT CONNECTOR

1. Quoted in Alison Flood, "Cain's Jawbone: TikTok Helps Reissued Literary Puzzle Fly off the Shelves," *The Guardian*, November 23, 2021. www.theguardian.com.

CHAPTER ONE: CONTENT CREATOR

2. Quoted in Maggie Butler, "How to Become a Content Creator: 10 Steps," *Hubspot*, September 6, 2023. www.blog.hubspot.com.

3. Quoted in Butler, "How to Become a Content Creator."

CHAPTER TWO: SOCIAL MEDIA MANAGER

4. Quoted in Hugo Molinaro, "How to Measure Your ROI on Social Media Marketing Campaigns," *Convince & Convert*, n.d. www.convinceandconvert.com.

5. Quoted in Julie Meredith, "The Power of Social Media to Capture Today's Consumer," *Forbes*, June 25, 2020. www.forbes.com.

CHAPTER THREE: CUSTOMER SERVICE REPRESENTATIVE

6. Quoted in "37 Percent of Consumers Trust Social Media Influencers over Brands," *Oracle*, May 3, 2022. www.prnewswire.com.

CHAPTER FOUR: DIGITAL FORENSICS INVESTIGATOR

7. Quoted in "Why Playing Capture the Flag Will Make You a Cyber Elite," *Booz Allen Hamilton*, n.d. www.boozallen.com

INDEX

IMAGE CREDITS

Cover: © Tirachard Kumtanom/Shutterstock Images
4: © Red Line Editorial
5: © Red Line Editorial
7: © Nikita Wayhome/Shutterstock Images
9: © Tada Images/Shutterstock Images
10: © Zamrznuti Tonovi/Shutterstock Images
13: © SeventyFour/Shutterstock Images
17: © Frame Stock Footage/Shutterstock Images
18: © Eugenio Marongiu/Shutterstock Images
21: © amenic181/Shutterstock Images
22: © HauLar/Shutterstock Images
25: © Rawpixel.com/Shutterstock Images
29: © goodluz/Shutterstock Images
30: © Rawpixel.com/Shutterstock Images
32: © PeopleImages.com-Yuri A/Shutterstock Images
34: © ronstik/Shutterstock Images
37: © Zurijeta/Shutterstock Images
39: © Rawpixel.com/Shutterstock Images
42: © fizkes/Shutterstock Images
44: © Ground Picture/Shutterstock Images
47: © Microgen/Shutterstock Images
50: © Felipe Caparros/Shutterstock Images
52: © Gorodenkoff/Shutterstock Images
55: © Krysja/Shutterstock Images
58 (top): © Natee Meepian/Shutterstock Images
58 (bottom): © Rawpixel.com/Shutterstock Images
59 (top): © DC Studio/Shutterstock Images
59 (bottom): © Kateryna Onyshchuk/Shutterstock Images

ABOUT THE AUTHOR

With a background in education, Roxanne Troup writes books that entertain, educate, and inspire young people. She lives in the mountains of Colorado with her family and enjoys visiting schools to promote literacy.